You're Not a Boob

By

MARK A. CRAYMER

You're Not a Boob

The story of a soon to be father and how
one event changed his life for ever

By

MARK A. CRAYMER

Order this book online at www.trafford.com
or email orders@trafford.com

Most Trafford titles are also available at major online book retailers.

Printed in the United States of America.

ISBN: 978-1-4269-6842-6 (sc)
ISBN: 978-1-4269-6843-3 (e)

Trafford rev. 05/02/2011

 www.trafford.com

North America & international
toll-free: 1 888 232 4444 (USA & Canada)
phone: 250 383 6864 ♦ fax: 812 355 4082

Dedication:

To my beloved wife Mindy and our new baby girl McKenzie Faith Craymer, with all my love and all that I have, I will always be yours and will cherish our life together always and forever.

PREFACE

The purpose of this book was to share my experiences of having a child. Many times, people think that they need to read every literary text to help provide a foundation as to how to raise a newly born child. The truth is you need love, willingness, and a lot of energy. During my wife's first pregnancy, we went looking at all of the books and trying to figure out what we needed to know, when all was said and done, we found that some tips worked and some did not. Ultimately, we decided that we would take things as they came. We realized that every pregnancy and child is different. So the best way to succeed is by simply taking things as they come. There is no philosophy, experience, or doctorate backing my experience, it is simply just one experience and how I handled these experiences.

The best advice I can give a new father is be patient, love whole heartedly, and work hard at being a good father. Remember this term is relative and as long as you love your family and are there for them, this is best first step you can take.

ACKNOWLEDGEMENTS

With writing this book, I have many people to thank and give my appreciation. First off, I am so blessed to have a wonderful wife. Mindy has provided me with a wonderful blessing in McKenzie and has been completely supportive of this book and has helped me to pursue dreams for which I would have never believed I could have done.

I also need to thank a wonderful friend Jeffery Ward, he has helped me in my preparation of this book and when all others provided discouragement in continuing this work, he brought forth a refreshing take on the work and has helped in reviewing and getting me to this stage. I appreciate his time, efforts and willingness to be my friend and take his time to help in this endeavor.

I also, need to thank Dr. Kirk Curnett- as a professor he was encouraging in my writing and helped me obtain the necessary skills to become the writer that I have become today. His willingness and experience in literary work has inspired me and I appreciate everything he has contributed to the success of this book by helping edit and proof it for me.

All of these people I hold dearly in my heart, for their abilities and willingness to uplift me and provide me the support in writing this book. Without support, it is difficult to meet your goals and dreams. I have been blessed to know each of these people and to have them be a part of my life. Without them, I would have never thought of taking on such an adventure.

INTRODUCTION

Too often when thinking about where life is heading and what the future holds the thoughts of becoming a father or parent are far from any man's mind until his wife says "It's Time." We all think that this comment simply means dinner's ready, sex, Monday Night Football, or bedtime. Never has the thought of fatherhood, parenting, child rearing, babies, dirty diapers, crying, late nights, exhaustion, and nursing come into mind. In fact, feeding time for most guys mean they get to eat; well, guys, these terms now mean a lack of football, lack of sex, and no more boob for you. Of course, of the many dreams and goals set by men, normally having kids is nowhere near the top of their list. In fact, at the age of five through fifteen while most girls are thinking of marriage and the perfect wedding, many boys are thinking of when his monster ramp will be built and when he will be able to start jumping the front yard ditch with his souped-up BMX bike. While racing down the street, he thinks to himself this will be the greatest and most risk taking jump in the history of bike jumps, what an awesome event. He will clear the five-foot ditch and world-wide records will be set. While soaring through the air, he ponders how glorious life is, and when the quick landing is a perfect stick, no boy thinks about the repercussions caused by the change in his voice and his lack of feeling between his legs. At that moment, producing kids is far from his mind; if it was, he probably just ended any possible chance of having them. In a high, squeaky voice and a little wobble in his step, he moves through the front yard and quickly realizes that both tires are blown on his magnificent dirt bike and that any balls he once had may too be just as deflated and lacking when performance is needed later in life. In looking back on life some other attributes that young men lack is even the willingness to state that they like girls. Most of the time, boys are too interested in the next adventure which will take them to new heights like scooping frogs or crawdads out of a nearby stream or sewer pipe. Even better, most boys treat girls at this age as the evil monster trying to attack the tree house castle. To succeed, they must capture the beast and lock them in the dungeon. This will prove their ability to reign supreme. That is at least in their earlier years. The sad part is guys already have a good picture of what married life is going to be like. The problem is they are the ones locked up and caged, no longer the dreamers, but instead crushed and chained in their new life, marriage.

At the age of fifteen through twenty, a man's goals and dreams start to develop and change. As love has struck the air and the girl becomes a beauty instead of a beast. Still, the man wants to lock the girl up, but at this point it is not for beheading but instead to caress and go goo-goo all over. At this point, the man has started developing his next stage, which basically declares him whipped and no longer in control. He has seen the hot cheerleader and desires having her as his wife or girlfriend along with dreaming of becoming the popular sports jock and legend that he always knew he was; meanwhile, the girls are once again thinking about how nice it would be to find a decent guy with whom they can have their perfect wedding with and have at least three children. Although as time goes on, some women change their mind about the three children now they want four or five. But remember once you say "I Do," you are not only stuck in an never ending, nagging situation, but now you get to hear someone else crying and screaming in the background.

So guys, this is the sign that you are heading to fatherhood. It maybe one, two, three, or if you are lucky five years, but you have just signed your life away and the simple life is gone.

Yes, I have been married five years and from the day of the wedding, I have been making one excuse after another of trying to get financially sound, paying off debt, getting out of school, and that the time was just not right. Of course, in a man's mind, without a boat, a Lake House, a million dollars, and visiting at least half a dozen different football stadiums, the time is never right for children. Guys, all I can say is that I have been drafted and those simple words "It's Time" have rung through to my ears. I am guessing that in reading this book something similar has happened to you, and now you are looking for some advice as to how to handle the upcoming events and the areas in which you will soon be facing. All I can say is hang on and here are a few tips that I have learned along the way. Granted many of them are things you will hear from others and guaranteed to be told by your mother (and of course your mother-in-law). Just remember that there are key things to remember in order to succeed, and you will not succeed the first time. This is a marathon not a sprint and there is no getting out once you have gotten into it. Finally, remember that having children isn't the end of the world just the end of your life as you know it.

Contents

CHAPTER ONE

The Clock Is Ticking

Throughout my life all I have heard from women all around is how precious the time is when having children. Although this seems great for women, we men would rather have nothing to do with it. In fact, the only age problem or clock ticking that we hear is the time spent at in-laws, watching chick flicks, and having to do chores around the house. Many times as these things are being done in our lives all we can think about is when it will be over, I wonder who won the game, or what's to eat.

Women go through most of their life wondering when their biological clock will run out and if they will be able to experience the enjoyment and fulfillment of having children. When my wife came to me and started asking about having children, I continually asked her. "Are you sure that you are ready?" Of course, this was my opportunity to extend our freedom and lack of having something that would prevent us from being able to live life to the fullest—or so I thought.

So far, I have lasted for five years, but one day the time came that I no longer could convince her we needed more time, in fact she was ready and her clock was not only ticking but it was chirping out loud. After many years of being on the pill and no longer having that safety net, the nerves and sweats start to overcome you as you think that with one slight slip, I have knocked her up and the real fun begins. Of course, the sex is great and the time spent with one another is something to look forward to, but the end result by far was the part that neither of us was quite ready for!

Over the past five years we have been pressured by family and friends of when we would start having children. In fact, your mother has probably already started stating that "I will never become a grandmother." Don't fall for it; it is just a ploy to get you and your wife to think about having a child. In fact, many times your parents are possibly only in their mid to late fifties and you think if life is almost over then I am over half way there. Yep, once you start thinking about this your wife will start thinking, oh no, my biological clock is running out. All this means guys is that no matter where you are in your relationship and life, the game is over and now growing up becomes a requirement no longer a luxury. In fact, I have heard it all from parents and siblings. We were fortunate we have a total of ten siblings between the two of us. Did I say fortunate? I meant cursed. Yes, some are whole, half, and even step, but that is another story all in itself. We have been hounded for the past few years of when they will be Aunts, Grandparents, Great Grandparents, etc. Throughout this time, you ponder; I wonder how long one can last without having to take that plunge. For some, it is immediate and sure enough you are having enjoyed your last sensual moment with your wife for at least nine months. Other times, you are able to prolong having kids by her either taking the pill, patch, or some "Y" thing they would like you to test out and it has an accuracy rate of 99%. No one really asks what about that 1%? If that doesn't scare you, now your wife wants you to attend all of her doctor's appointments. At this point, you are wondering if it is ever enough. I have to see her when I come home, when she is in the mood, and for the rest of my life. Do I also have to see some other man having to look at it and then explain to me how it supposedly works? I mean give us a break already, it is bad enough that we have to hear you tell us when we can have it, for how long, and what position, but now having a man describe it to us, this is just embarrassing.

If this does not bother you, the realizations of how many alternatives and contraceptives that can be taken by women are absolutely just ridiculous. These are all wonderful, but shortly after that you start to hear your wife state, does she look fat? Of course, the answer is always no, but let's be honest sometimes we all think differently but if you express what you really think you don't have to worry about kids, you will be lucky to still be married. When my wife started taking the pill, her comments were, "I feel bloated, fat, and no longer attractive." What she really is saying is can I come off of this thing and you take something. Although many women will never admit it, if they could they would make men have the children. In fact, every time I would sit beside my wife while she was pregnant you could hear her question who was the pregnant one. What I told her was I was gaining weight so that she did not feel so bad about her weight gain. What really gets bad is when you see other people stare at you and it is noticeable that what they really are thinking, is what a sympathetic husband; he gained weight for his wife who looks like a whale. It is hilarious to watch people come up to a pregnant woman and state you look wonderful. I mean if I gained 30 pounds my wife would be screaming Weight Watchers!

So once you get past the doctor's appointments, lack of sex, the PMS cycles, and now the weight gain you start questioning whether or not her figure will ever be what it once was and if her mood swings will ever stop. Although her clock is no longer ticking, the bell has just rang and you are about to go 18 rounds without any padding or protection from her hormones. The sad news is this is already happening without her being pregnant. Just think about what the next 9 months are going to be like, you will have no free time, no sports, many doctor's visits, cold and hot flashes from when she decides to turn the air conditioner on to that when she states she is cold and when she then she will heat you to death other nights. In other words, it will feel like you are up on Mt. Everest trying to survive from hypothermia and then other times it will feel like you are in a volcano whether it be the temperature or just her mood, no matter what you cannot get away quick enough and time just cannot go by fast enough.

CHAPTER TWO

Who's the Father?

After seeing the changes and the reactions of your sweet innocent bride, you have to ask "Who's the Father." Of course, the answer is simple and no you are not asking if she has been cheating on you. The simple question is asked because at no point were you thinking this moment would come so quickly and yes how can we reverse this transaction. Although the above may all be true, the fact sometimes is relevant in terms of asking especially in the type of society we live in. The problem with asking a question like this is you will be sleeping on the couch for the full 9 months and yes whatever pain she is feeling you will feel it ten times worse. My suggestion is leave this question alone and follow the advice below. Love her, cherish her, and whatever you do don't go to sleep with her angry at you, you may wake up with body parts missing. At this point not many men expect this process to be very difficult or be something that comes out of a horror flick, but let me tell you there are precious moments and sometimes let's just say stay at work pull up a cot and don't go home.

Of course, I am kidding, not! You have just reached the final and it is due or die time! Finding out that your wife is pregnant is quite an experience. In looking back, first, you thought buying tampons was an embarrassing experience, wait until you get to the store and are having to buy fifty different types of pregnancy tests. As you go through with your sun glasses and trench coat on walking down the isle of women's care goods, you quickly look both ways and grab each kind. The reason for this is you want to make sure that she cannot fool you and that the signs are very evident. Well, so you think. Once you have crossed over and started buying women supplies you are definitely no longer considered a bachelor much less a man. As you approach the checkout counter you notice that the cashier is a hot young blonde who is going to look at you in one of two ways. First she will either think you are sweet and a good husband or second she will look at you as a pervert and think that you are whipped. Of course, in my experience it was an older women, who of course at that point with her sly and squinting eyes looks at you as if she cannot tell what it is at first and then she states what a nice young man you are. Meanwhile she starts giving you and your wife advice in line on how to use it and what are the best ways to pee on a stick. Either way, your reputation is shot and you will no longer be looked at as a man.

Once you get home and now are extremely embarrassed by the whole experience, you then have to sit down with your wife and read the instructions. Of course, some of the symbols can be quite tricky. Most of the units come with a plus or minus sign and then is color coded so that you can tell whether or not she is pregnant. Others are easy and to the point, pregnant or not pregnant. I liked these; they were easy to read and seemed to never be wrong. Of course, we had to test three different times as if one time was not enough. Finally, the other alternative was the ones with multiple lines. These were very difficult to understand and what if only half a line showed up, what in the world does that mean?

After all the drama and the decision has been made on which one to use, your wife goes into the other room takes a few moments and don't ask how or what position she chooses, you really do not want to know. After a few more minutes and losing half of your finger nails you start to see what the results are. At this point, you are not certain what answer you want, but you definitely want an answer. Our first two times were negative, I was somewhat relieved when I read that, but in the end somewhat disappointed. As men, we normally do not have emotion in these types of areas and normally the excitement comes when it is always negative. Of course, our reaction stays within, but there is definitely a party going on inside us. As you console your wife, you find that those feelings eventually will affect you as well, but the time is not quite right yet.

After consoling your wife and the realization that you are not pregnant this is wonderful for you, you normally get the opportunity that night to fool around and try, try again. The greatest part about trying to have a baby is the chance to have more and more sex. At this point she is no longer giving you specific times, places, or positions, but instead she is encouraging more often, more times, and has become a wild maniac in trying new things. This is an exciting part of your marriage and yes you are definitely excited in working on getting her pregnant, but you forget that once this is all done you will only be placed back on ice and may never get to experience this wonderful act ever again.

Throughout marriage you will find many things that change your feelings, emotions, and views of your wife, but this beats them all. The excitement of having a new born child and adding to your family is fun at the beginning. You start looking at some ideas for a nursery, you get gifts, and you get the opportunity to enjoy a sacred experience with someone you love. It is a great period for you and your wife, but it has only been the first month and nothing has changed. During the first few months it is exciting and a new experience for the both of you. Your little one is slowly growing inside your wife's belly and soon will develop into what I will later call your little devil.

As time creeps along, you find that going to the doctor's is getting easier; your wife's appetite is getting bigger which of course you like. More food for her means more food for you, or so you think. In fact, the simple truth to the whole experience is that you actually get more benefit than what you originally expect. You can now blame the fact of going out to favorite restaurants and eating fattening foods is good for you and her, I mean the ideas and thoughts that run through your head are ice cream, pizza, pickles, peanut butter, and other huge cravings for which your wife will definitely want to enjoy. With this, it gives you an opportunity to enjoy and fill up on all the great foods and experiences that is unless you have a wife like mine. I was looking forward to all the free food and the Mexican night cravings, but instead all she could mustard was fruit and more fruit. She would tell me that her cravings were to eat more naturally; you know fruits, vegetables, and the occasional dairy product hog wash! She just was holding me back and preventing me from having the night on the town, I was almost certain of that.

As time continues, you start realizing that this is your baby and soon you will have a huge responsibility. You know nothing yet.

CHAPTER THREE

The Hump

After the first month, you start thinking this has been easy there is no way this can get much harder. I mean you have gone through the stress of finding out whether or not you and your wife our pregnant. Then later you confirm that you are and yes your wife loves you and you are the father. Well the one thing that most men are not prepared for is the hump.

In fact, the truth to the matter is simple, with every day that passes the hump only gets larger and larger. After the first month the stage is a simple one, your wife starts to look pudgier of course do not tell her this, her hormones are off the Richter scale. In fact, as you look closely her belly is turning into a doughnut and looks to have wrinkles forming all around. This is somewhat disturbing and your just glad it is not summer and she is wherein a bikini or sports bra. The sight is quite overwhelming and in fact soon becomes more than you can possibly handle. The thoughts that run through your mind are she is so beautiful when I married her and that was if she was ever beautiful in the beginning and at least to you, but now look at her she is gaining weight like a sumo wrestler and soon her underwear will be like thongs when they really are suppose to be full support.

One positive trait that most men like when their wife starts to have changes is the increase in the boob area. Although for smaller women it is not as much and for larger women you can no longer tell the difference between their bust and their belly, if you have the perfect racked women with good size and she keeps her weight to a healthy minimum, you will be one happy man. In my case, I felt I had a beautiful wife from the beginning. And no, I am not just saying that! She truly was a very beautiful woman when I married her. As time went by we both have got a little larger, but as a pregnant five foot one inch and three quarters woman she did not have much room between her torso and head to accommodate her already double "D" bust and now her sixty-five inch waist. Just kidding, it just seems that large but really is not. The sad news, men do not joke on your wives weight or size because if you are anything like me you will end up being embarrassed.

To explain more, you find one more interesting part about having children is the ability to once again get free things. With showers and family offerings the getting is very good. In fact, the showers are the best part of the pregnancy period. We are blessed, remember we have ten siblings, this means the gifts come from many areas. Of course, the other side of this is simply at showers the most expected event done are games. Yes guys you helped make the baby you should get to participate in the showers. Normally because you are whipped and your wife makes you but seriously why not enjoy in the fun. This gets me back to my embarrassing story. I joked to my wife for months about how much larger she was getting. I mean I thought she had some type of pump and ball under that waist. Every morning when I woke up she just seemed to get larger and larger. In fact,

I believed through the night she would sit there and deflate her belly by pulling the plug and in the morning she pumped it back up but did not remember how big so she added a few extra pounds of air. So, with playing games at showers, yes, you will be embarrassed. At this particular shower we were asked to pull from a roll of plastic ribbon a length that would be the circumference of the entire belly from belly button to the small of the back. Well, I thought I would be funny and measured my waist. It was going to be hilarious, I would then prove that my wife was in fact getting fat and now was bigger than I was. Of course, this did not go exactly as planned. I pulled the tape out and wrapped it around my waist; afterwards I cut the line and dangled it in front of me. It looked to be almost as tall as my wife, but I knew I was on track. As she came closer, I realized that my string was way too long and that it needed to be cut shorter. As she approached, I quickly cut the string and put it to her waist, almost a perfect match. I think after all said and done it measured to 33" well afterwards I remembered removing the additional and subtracted that from my normal waste. Let's just say I no longer joked on my wife's weight. Instead I quietly withdrew most comments and sat myself down. Humiliating at nine months pregnant, I was still much larger than my wife. So guys take my advice love your wife and encourage her, but unless you are skinny like a bean pole, you may find yourself sticking your foot in your mouth like I did.

Now that you know I am a healthy (fat) man, you now can picture this. After finding out we were pregnant and that between my size and my wife's soon to be size our simple queen bed would just not suffice for our everyday or every night needs. We decided to get a king—size bed for this new adventure. Remember that when your wife's hump fully develops is looks like a big butter ball. Let's just say you need the room. Thinking about butter balls, this reminds me I have finally figured out where the term butter ball comes from. It was always believed that when someone was called a butter ball it means they are fat, well I beg to differ. I believe this term was coined off the idea based for pregnant women. The reason for this conclusion is around three months; you start to hear the doctor state that to help with the stretch marks your wife will need to start creaming her belly. The interesting substance which you will later find out is called "Cocoa Butter Cream." Men this stuff is exactly like it sounds. It is a thick, yellow, and smells like sun bathing lotion. When applied it coats like butter on your wife's belly and soon you find that it coats almost to anything. Once applied anything that lands on her belly comes across that cream and slides right off. I mean one night if you are cooking and you find that you are missing oil or butter, just scoop some off and fry up your chicken with that stuff because it is slippery and just like butter. Don't worry, if you needed to slide down a hill and get away from something fast just turn your wife face down and go, you will have a heck of a boogey board.

Like I was saying, your life is over with when having children. In the early days, you possibly once got a massage here or there, now every night your wife is asking if you can apply her butter cream to her thighs, waist, back, and all other parts which are stretching from the massive fluid being retained and from the growth of the baby. If this was not bad enough, now you have to attend to the normal everyday cleaning. As the hump gets larger, the first doctor's visit is not too bad he just states that she needs to take life easier and with less stress and pressure. By the second visit he is stating that your wife is no longer able to carry anything heavier than 10-20 pounds and should not be doing any major lifting or moving. Later in other visits he then adds more restrictions; he states no more sweeping, vacuuming, or using harsh chemicals. This means now as the husband you are no longer watching TV but cleaning, cooking, washing clothes and all house chores. Why do you think this, well the clothes now weigh more than 10 pounds, the vegetable oil is considered a harsh chemical, and lifting simply means getting out of a chair. I mean granted she has gained a lot of weight at this point but you only thought she was selective and nit picking, now everything is literally too much and must be done by you. While growing up you always watched those movies where the husband is running around and losing all this weight, this is because he now works a full time job, is a stay at home maid at night, and butler/chef while his wife is taking power naps.

Men, again your life is over and you have only reached five months. By month six, she wants to start looking for all the cute baby clothes because now you know what it is going to be, suggestion here, find out what the sex of the baby will be it is much easier. In addition to searching for clothes it is now time to start talking about bed room colors, fixtures, furniture, and construction of the room completely. Yes, let me comment on this. Guys you only thought you had finished your to do list, well expect a whole new list. In this case, when having a child your list grows by leaps and bounds. If you are anything like me and do not have the money to hire it out to be done, you will be doing it yourself. So all of you do it yourselfers, I have been there, run and hide.

So moving on, now that you have decided what color to paint the room, you start working; at this point she starts to ponder and wants chair molding, special wallpaper trim, and special features like a giraffe switch plate. In addition to this, she wants to go and buy protective gear. No not helmets, pads, or anything we can associate with, she wants plug inserts, foam for the fireplace, cabinet locks. I mean the baby is not even out of the womb and you are already locking up all the china and glassware and preparing your house for sound proof and the world wind of destruction to hit. Finally, once you have the house all bubble like and ready to start preventive measures of when the war between you and the baby begins. Now, you find yourself shopping whether actually buying something or just looking at the same things three times a week. Throughout the pregnancy she will continue to state honey, I want to go walking, but when you get out she really just wanted to make a pit stop at the local Dairy Queen for some ice cream, her mid afternoon snack before supper, second supper, third supper, and a bed time snack.

If you only understood then what you do now, things would have been so much clearer. Yes, she eats if not eight times at least five to seven times a day. In fact, no wonder she looks like a beached whale. Again, remember do not say it to her face for all you will encounter is possibly a loss of skin, or in some cases decapitation of body parts. At this point hormones are blaring and screaming, so do nothing to tick her off. By month seven, things seem to have settled a little and it has only been three months without sex at this point. She is still cranky and yes you want to stay at work, but you still find yourself going home cooking dinner and those things that seemed so bad in months five and six are starting to become less and less of a strain. At this point, you are starting to become more comfortable with the nightly creaming and find that even your hands are starting to look silky from all the lotion you have to use. It does not start hitting you that you no longer are playing or watching sports, and simply enjoying the comradely of your fellow gentlemen. You have now officially become a whipped man and can no longer call yourself a manly man.

During the seventh month, you now are starting the Lamaze classes and Breastfeeding classes. I can say these are not as bad as you would think. Before we started, I thought, great the breast feeding class will be women surrounding me with pulling their breast out and discussing on how to properly insert it in a plastic dolls mouth. The bad part about this class is you will not find any hot chicks in these classes. Remember they are all pregnant and massive. Although this class was only for one night, I felt very awkward in going into a room full of strangers and describe my wife's breast and how she should have to hold it in order to feed the baby. This is just not done! Guys it is not that bad, you watch a film and to be honest it basically describes everything we already knew. I mean come on whom better to ask how to suck on a boob than a man? We all know that men from an early age understand the concept of the birds and bees, let's be honest we grew up on a boob and throughout our entire married life when allowed are attached to one throughout intercourse. This is our specialty. Guys by the time your wife makes it to seven months, you are no longer getting any and simply put, no boob for you.

Later, after attending breast feeding class and realizing that if your wife struggles you are an expert, you now have to learn how to soothe your wife in Lamaze. I have always seen TV shows where people are going to Lamaze and breathing, I never could see myself looking like a hyper hyena, but it is amazing what love for your wife and threatening from your wife will do. In fact, lying down on the mats and listening to solemn music is not terrible especially if you get a snooze in between. Overall the class is well scripted and provides a great way of relaxing. Just remember, on the day of delivery, that you are suppose to be the one relaxing her not yourself. I made that mistake some during the class and probably enjoyed the relaxing sessions way too much. Also guys, if none of the above excited you, remember they do give out free stuff. Of course the items are not considered guy stuff, but considering you would have to buy it, it is still cool to get. So if you go for no other reason other than for the relaxation and free stuff, you should support your wife, so just do it.

As we move out of the seven month, the eighth month your wife now has to turn sideways to go through most doors. At the same time the car is now balanced instead of leaning to your side, the weight and water pressure will start to get to her. This only means one thing, more massages and more work for you. Now that you are in eighth month, you are so ready for the baby to come out that you start to think will it ever get here. The comments start from your wife, would you love me if I am fat starts to fill the air. It of course is also ringing true, but do not share this. Of course, your wife misses the fact that if it was only the fat that bothers you would be one thing, but between her getting fat, eating like a pig, and passing bodily sounds like a man, I do not think so. Yes, the bodily functions of a woman are now truly showing. For example, one day I took my wife to lunch with a friend of ours. While sitting there, we were ordering and after the friend and I ordered, we realized that my wife was still deciding on what to order for her meal. While listening, it was some camp stew, some more camp stew, and lima beans. Of course, knowing that this would not suffice for an eight month due pregnant women, I stated she could share some of mine when it came out. After getting our meal, she had cleared her entire plate, started eating some of my fries, and finishing some of my chicken. When the waitress came by to ask if we were done, the friend and I stated sure and she started to take our plates, my wife lunges at her and states "you can't have this yet" and grabs my plate. Of course, with the fierce eye and the magnitude of the lunge, both I and our friend sat back and told the waitress it is ok she doesn't bite and I finally calmed my wife down. Guys that day was a scary day for all mankind, whether it was the hormones, hunger, or simply that she was becoming ravenous, all I can say I no longer touch my wife's plate until asking her if she is done for fear of losing a finger or my life. Everything changes with a pregnancy, all of the innocence you once knew from your wife has now been lost and she has been replaced by a beast.

Of course, things become funny after looking back, but during those times, you start wonder what happened to the woman you married. Finally, during the ninth month, she starts wondering will this pregnancy ever be over and you both wonder will life ever be back to what it once was. The answer is no and no. Life will never be the same and neither will anything else you once cherished and desired. During this last month preparations are almost finished and all of your hard labor and work in the baby's room will start to show and the final touches will be made at this time. The packing for the hospital and arrangements are started and you set up where and when you will be arriving and finalize these arrangements. This is whether or not you go into labor. The interesting part about the time before the birth, I always imagined that our birthing experience would turn out like the movie "Nine Months." The water would break and as we are going into labor she is screaming and hollering, I would be driving down the street and as I am passing street by street the likelihood of running someone over and having to take them to hospital would also be necessary. Finally, when reaching the hospital, I would jump out to fetch my wife and put her in a wheel chair all at the same time running up and down the halls of hospital ranting that she is having a baby. Finally, once getting her in, they would have to provide me with a sedative and put me on the bed next to her. Of course none of this happened to me, but don't be to certain it can't happen to you. No, as the last few weeks started coming to an end all sort of things run through your mind and the questions which you will never have answers too, start to arise. These questions normally go something like this, what will you wear, when will it come, what does water breaking look like, if it breaks on the carpet do you clean before you go or just go, will there be a lot of screaming, what happens if the baby is starting to come out before you get to the hospital, and trust me I can go on for hours. Let's just say, I thought I was a pretty level minded man, but these questions just keep popping into your head and no matter what questions you come up with, everything will be alright. Whatever you do, unless it is agreed upon by your wife and yourself before you go into the delivery room, make sure it was ok with her to video or take pictures. If not, that question is better never asked and you do not want to know the answer.

CHAPTER FOUR

The Birthing Incident

Finally, the time has come to share in the blessed event of having a baby. Did I say blessed, let's just say nightmare and the worse horror flick I have ever seen. It was like watching *"Alien"* where Sigourney Weaver is being stretched from the inside out and you can see the movement then all of a sudden something pops out of her stomach and starts to screech and as it climbs out, it is covered with slime and goo and literally you're so overwhelmed in the experience that you are sitting on the edge of your seat. Well, guys, it is about as interesting as this, but before you were unable to take your eyes off the experience this time you will hope to never see that experience again. Before I get into more detail let me tell you how my experience went and then you can only imagine how yours might go.

It all started about three days before the actual birth of my daughter. My wife and I had gone out for a bit of shopping and picking up some groceries for when we got out of the hospital with the new baby. As we were driving back home, I had noticed on the side of the street a light pole from where our power company had come and swapped over our existing pole.

Not much to look at and never would have thought it to be a problem. As we walk into our house, it looked as if Armageddon had just struck the house and the light flickered as if from a scene from poltergeist. The fans were racing as if they had been put onto hyper speed and the lights when turned on were like looking at a nuclear blast that had just gone off. As we were searching for answers, we realized quickly that something must be wrong and shut down all circuit breakers in our house. After a brief moment, I was able to conclude that when reconnecting our power lines the power company must have crossed the wrong lines and instead of sending 200 Volts of electricity to our box, they were sending up to 1000 Volts. Let's just say they were burning our house down from the inside out and if given any more time it would have been crispier than a piece of chicken. If that was not bad enough, we had just been to the doctor three days before to find out that we would be scheduled for admittance into hospital on the next Sunday and we were now facing a house made of charcoal and barbequed appliances. After finally getting the power company out to fix the crossed wires, we found that our bed (Sleep Number), baby monitors, freezer, alarm radio clock, and humidifiers had all been fried. So you can only imagine that with three days before going into the hospital to have an induced labor, we were now facing the need of having to get all of these items repaired or fixed. So between the electrical company coming out fixing our house and sending us a check, we managed to accomplish replacing everything in the house that had been damaged, we were able to get all items fixed the day before having to go into the hospital. Of course, we thought this experience was bad enough but it only gets more interesting of a story from here out.

Finally, the day arrives and we check into the hospital, we find that the staff in the hospital is nice and that we were able to reserve the delivery room we wanted. All was going perfectly as planned. After getting settled into the hospital we were visited by family and were able to spend some quality time before visiting hours were over. At this point everything is going well, guys; here is where things get much more interesting for you especially. After visiting hours were over, we started getting prepared for the night ahead. As I was looking around for somewhere to sleep, I found that the couch was probably the best location to start off with. As I laid down I could hear every bone in my body cry out for my bed, the surface looked comfortable but it was like laying on a concrete floor which had a thin sheet on it. To make things worse it was also narrow and shorter than it looked. In fact, the couch length maybe was about five foot long and two and one half feet wide, well we covered the fact early that I am a heavier set guy and I stand about six feet tall, so I am now laying on a short, narrow, lumpy piece of concrete and with little to no blanket. As I laid there and thought, with one slight turn, I would end up on the hard-wood floor inside the hospital and who knows what types of germs there might be lying awaiting my arrival. If it only would get better, after sleeping for about an hour, I heard the door crack and it was the nurse refilling my wife's saline bag. Then after another hour passed she was back again and again. This went on and on throughout the night. Finally the next morning at 4 a.m. the doctor comes in to bust the water, guys this is the term where the sack around the baby is considered a water sack, he popped it, and when he did you would had thought rotten eggs were for breakfast. The smell was horrible and just lingered. Let's put it this way, if the honeymoon was not over before you came into this room, it is now. You get to see many different parts of your wife and the smell is definitely not a turn on. Even after this episode you may have an experience like me and have to hold a pan under your wife to allow her to pee, once they pop the bag there is no going back now. At this point, you are stuck and if the nurse is not available, guess what; you are now responsible for the cleanup. As the day progressed we noticed that the room seemed to get warmer and warmer. At around six that morning, I got up and checked the thermostat. It was set on 70 degrees, but it felt like 80. After a little more time passed, it just seemed to get hotter and hotter. Finally my wife was feeling the pain of the baby moving and started getting warm herself. After a few minutes, I went to the front desk and stated our problem of the room getting warmer, I mean women get hormones, us men are not suppose to feel that, are we? Therefore after about an hour it was told to us that the AC was broken and that they would attempt to get it fixed as quickly as possible. As sweat was rolling down my cheek, I spent most of the morning providing ice chips and cold rags for my wife's face, but no matter how much we attempted to beat the heat, it was just too much to bear. Shortly after, I was graciously brought breakfast, between the heat, the smell, and the lack of sleep I barely got the food down. Within minutes a sickness feel over me and nausea set in, soon after I was visiting the bathroom and losing my breakfast. Although I wanted to be strong for my wife, I too was struggling with the heat and lack of sleep, thereby deciding to go home and get a fan to assist with the heat of the room and hopefully help with the nausea we both were feeling.

As I was driving home to go get the fan, I could only imagine that she would have the baby without me there, luckily we only lived a few miles away, so I was able to quickly get back. After getting back, I was able to set up the fan and with the problems we had a few days back I could only think "Murphy" has sought us out. To share a little, throughout my life Murphy's Law has always played a role in my life. If it is going to happen it would happen to me. So far, everything was going wrong and there was nothing I could do. As the time passed, it was about mid day, we had made a pact not to allow anyone into the room and that the experience would be only for the two of us. The contractions were getting worse and I could only imagine that soon we would be experiencing some real pain. Of course, with our preconceived notion of not allowing anyone in the room, we were visited by virtually every family member and as they showed up we pointed them to the waiting room. Finally, the time had come, the contractions were getting closer and closer and so were the beats of my heart. As the nurses were starting to prepare her for delivery, they stated the doctor was on his way, all I could think is great I am going to have to deliver this baby or at least participate more than just being a coach. As time grew, so did the contractions, they were getting closer and closer together and the doctor still had not shown himself. Finally, the head nurse turned and started having my wife push. As I watched, I could see a black ball like tip sticking out. At that moment, I wondered what I have gotten myself into. As my nerves and heart were maxed out, I stood there holding one of my wife's legs as she would push. Encouraging and support are not even the right words for what we were experiencing. To go through this experience you must really love each other and more so you must really want children. After a few minutes of pushing, I could see more of the head and just sat back in awe as to how in the world there would soon be a little person in our midst. Finally, it was around 4:45 p.m. on that Monday, October 20, 2008, and the doctor had arrived. I walked out to let everyone in the waiting room know that she was pushing and was doing well. Before going out, the doctor had started getting prepared for delivery and unless he could get the baby out within a few moments my wife would end up having to have an emergency "C" section. After telling this news, I stepped back into the room and as the doctor worked on his part, I sat there encouraging my wife waiting for her to grab an appendage of my body and swear at me. At this point, I was lucky the drugs had taken their effect and she barely knew I was there. The pain must have been severe, but I could only imagine what it would have been like without any drugs for me and her.

After about ten minutes, the doctor started to cut away parts of skin around the private parts of my wife, of course I thought it would never be the same again. As he finished, she pushed a few more times and the baby was born at 4:55 p.m. In amazement, I watched how the head of my child had squeezed its way out of my wife and as one shoulder and then the next and finally the torso and then the legs came out, I was shocked to see how an 8 pound 15 oz. baby could have ever fit into my wife of five foot one inch. This was definitely an amazing event as it unfolded, but yet it was not over. As I stood watching my child and wife, I could see the doctor start pulling something else out while cutting the umbilical cord. Of course, the first thing that crosses your mind is great they miscounted; well as to my surprise he was attempting to pull what is called the afterbirth out. As he brought my daughter out she had a head that was oblong and coned at the top, just like Dan Aykroyd in *Cone Heads*. While watching the doctor continue working down at the foot of my wife's bed, I noticed that the umbilical cord was like a slinky that had been stretched out and if the baby wanted to she could have just bungeed right out of her mother's belly and would have sprung right back up. After waiting and watching the afterbirth, it was like an oval round purple egg that was all slimy and covered with a film. This was truly something right out of a horror flick, the term Alien was right on the end of my tongue. After ten stitches he was able to close up my wife and at that point, I was almost interested in stating don't you just want to say enough no more children, but I quickly held my tongue. The experience was one I had never seen and although it could have been worse, I felt that it was one of the most perfect days of my life. Even though the smell, heat, electricity problems, and even the nausea had set in, I could not have believed it to be any better than what I actually experienced.

After the birth, the cleaning process of the baby was quite interesting. They sucked the nose and mouth out with a vacuum like hose, and I figured they had a Viking on the other end. After words, they stamped my daughters feet on a card signed by her nurse and doctor and gave her back to my wife. An hour later we were moved downstairs and setup for the evening in recovery. As we were setting up for recovery, the baby was bathed and taken to the nursery for her first diaper change and to have the umbilical cord inked. After about twenty minutes she was brought to the room and everyone who had waited in the waiting room joined for the first time experiencing our new born child. Although your experience may be different, I hope the outcome is the same. By the end you will have a new blessing and definitely an experience never to forget.

CHAPTER FIVE

The Day after Tomorrow

What an experience the day of delivery was. We went through the wringer and back, but still survived. After moving back into the recovery suite, I once again found that my lack of sleep was slowly but surely catching up with me. As I watched my new born child in her mother's arms, I watched the excitement and at the same time questioned "What Now!" We had spent the last nine months waiting for this event to take place and now that it has, is there any way to reverse the action and act like it never happened? Don't misunderstand me, I was truly in love with my daughter and the experience was by far the most enjoyable yet scariest experience of my life. The biggest problem at this point was that nothing had prepared me for what I soon would experience and the adventure I now was about to partake in.

Although the birthing experience was definitely a stomach turner and the thought of now having another person to be responsible for and take care of, this thought could not be removed from my mind. I sat and watched this wonderful being as she watched her new surroundings and experienced the warmth of having a new born life in my arms. This experience is definitely one you will never forget. After sitting there and watching all the family pour in and hold our new blessing, you start to wonder how life will be now. As previously mentioned we waited almost five years before having a child, we enjoyed our freedom of being able to go when and where we pleased having no other responsibility other than ourselves. Now we had this new little bundle and I am almost certain everything will change. After visitation ended for the evening, we elected to send the baby to the nursery. Guys, if you do nothing else, I encourage you to have the baby sent to the nursery while you are in the hospital. They feed, clean, and tend to all the babies needs while you attempt to sleep on a two foot by three foot laid out recliner. If you thought the couch in the delivery room was small, all I can say is the baby has more room in their cart then you do on the recliner. I think the purpose is for the father to experience what the baby had to experience for the last nine months cooped up inside the mother's belly. All I can say is even when curled like a baby in the womb the sleeping area is smaller, for the dad, in proportion of the baby and the belly and you and the recliner. You were lacking sleep before you came to the hospital now you will never catch up.

To make things worse, depending on how your wife does through her delivery you could have many different things happen while you attempt to sleep. In my situation, I was rudely awakened every hour on the hour for them to check my wife's blood pressure and to assist in making sure everything was going well. In addition to that, my wife did not help much, she was waking every other hour needing to use the bathroom and due to her issues in delivery she needed assistance in doing so. So you lose sleep from the nurse, then from the bladder of your wife, finally every three hours they bring the baby in for feeding. The funniest part about this, according to everyone you talk to, is the mother does not start producing milk that can be drank by the baby right away, but they do start producing colostrum. This is thick yellow mucus like substance which comes at first and then the milk starts to come in. Sounds like a treat, huh guys? So really the purpose of bringing the baby in is not for food but instead to establish the child on breast feeding. So guys, now you know you lose sleep, dignity, and now the enjoyment of your wife. Yes, having a baby already seems like you have given up more than anyone ever could. I mean sleep is one thing, but when you have to go in and help your wife use the bathroom, take a shower, and remove her diaper you start to wonder did you have only one baby or develop an epidemic and everyone in your life now needs to be take care and you now become the servant not the one being served.

After making it through the first night, you wake up, no correction you get up because you have not really slept all night and you start to drag yourself around the room making sure your wife is doing well and your baby has had a good first night in the world. At around dawn most of the commotion and interruptions which has been going on all night has calmed down, your wife is still sleeping and the baby has gone back to the nursery, at this moment you smell an odor that needs to be remedied and therefore, with no hesitation you leave to go refresh yourself before the morning truly begins. At this time, you have to make an intuitive decision of whether to drive home and take a shower or to just refresh in the sink within the room. As you decide to take a ride home, you get in the car and drive frantically home trying to make it back before anyone realizes you have gone. After making it home in five minutes or less, you strip while going to the bathroom even before you unlock the door. You step into the bath-tub and turn on the water of course it is freezing and you have no time for warmth to take hold. As you scramble through your bath you quickly rinse and before even drying off you climb into various clothes hoping that they match or at least complement in some form or fashion. After getting dressed, you quickly drive back to the hospital only to find that your wife has woken and has already eaten breakfast. After getting back you call the nursery to retrieve your baby and as you call you state that you would like to have the baby brought down for the remainder of the day. The baby at this time arrives and you start to work with your wife on helping her finish eating and provide means to take care of the baby. So far everything is going well, you may not exactly know what is going on or whether or not you are doing it right, but for now everything seems to be working and you have not completely lost your mind.

A few hours past, as you start to realize that you have not really eaten anything in a couple of days or at least it feels this way. As people come in and out of the room visiting, you find time to rejuvenate yourself by going and grabbing something to eat. I was lucky, there was a restaurant in the hospital for which we stayed, so I was able to leave the room and within minutes walk to get something, eat it and then walk back. Of course, as you are walking out of the room, you wonder how many eyes are staring at you thinking what a jerk to leave his wife and baby and go get something to eat, I have to say not many people think this, only you. The reason for this thought by you is from guilt for all of the times in which you have watched football or done something for which your wife was waiting on your sorry behind. Now it has all come back to haunt you. As you walk down, you think to yourself wow I am so glad for a break, but while you are gone all you can think about is whether or not your wife needs something or if the baby is being properly taken care of. In fact, for most of your meal and time walking back you can think of nothing else, but how quick you can get back to the room and make sure everything is going ok.

As you walk into the room, everyone wonders why you have only been gone for twenty minutes and they think that you should have taken more time, afterwards even you yourself are now thinking, wow I wish I would have enjoyed that sandwich or if you were like me, what did I eat? Of course, it didn't matter now, you have swallowed and there is no getting it back now. As time rolls on, you have many visitors that come and see the baby; some are family, other co-workers, and finally some friends. It is amazing who will come see you while you are in a hospital. While we were there, we were visited by our church's prayer minister and hospital coordinator. He came in, luckily my wife knew who he was, and I looked at him as to why would you be here? But as he sat down, you think to yourself how long will you be planning on staying, what is your purpose for being here, and what benefit do you get for coming to see us? All of these types of questions go through your mind, normally you would not mind, but at this point you are now like a rabid dog who has not slept, had very little to eat, and ready to bark and bite anything that comes in to prevent you or the baby from precious sleep.

Ok, I am being a little drastic. It is more like your mother-in-law visiting your home, when you did not invite her or she did not state she was coming. You get it now? Well this is how I felt with this intruder into our lives. After awhile he shortly left and life was back to normal. As others continued to come, you find yourself becoming more and more protecting of the baby and your wife. You start to make comments like, I think it is time for feeding or I think she needs rest, which of course gets more people out of the room or simply too leave. In my case, I had to deal with one mother, one mother-in-law, one step mother-in-law, one dad, one father-in-law, and ten siblings; so nevertheless, we were always having the room occupied. As the day started to creep on, we also found time to schedule a meeting with our lactation nurse, or for layman breast nurse. We were unable to meet with her the first day, but boy the next was a new experience not only for me, but my wife as well.

CHAPTER SIX

You're Not a Boob

Guys, it is true you never thought it would happen, but now you have competition and for that matter you are on the losing end of this battle. For months leading up to the birth of my child, I still every once in a while enjoyed the leisure of spending time with my wife. We would still fool around and I would still see some action towards getting some booby, but as soon as we met with the lactation nurse (booby nurse), I knew that this time was a thing of the past.

On our second day in the hospital, we stopped having bunches and bunches of visitors and started finding ourselves with more time on our hands to spend with our new born child. Early that morning, we were visited by the lactation nurse to discuss the various things new mothers go through as well new fathers. Of course, the main focus was on how to properly breast feed the baby. At this point, you start seeing the things you once enjoyed and played with being played with by another human being, your child. I have to admit, the once luscious and exciting parts of being able to play with your wife has now become a thing of the past, you start watching your wife play with herself and it no longer is a turn on, but something is coming out of it. I mean, this is truly disturbing and may not be for those weak in the stomach. As you sit there, you are finding out how your wife needs to pull and squeeze in order for your child to latch on. Afterwards you start to learn the holds for which the baby can be placed in to make it comfortable for the mother and child. This is interesting, because you thought there was only one hold and many positions, but as for feeding a baby, you start to hear about the various positions like a football hold, the cradle, and even the press. I made up the press, but geez they sure are pressed to that boob and barely can get air; yes you can be jealous now.

The purpose of these holds is for the mother to be able to hold the baby while comforting it. The football hold is literally like holding the baby like a football player would hold a football. The issue I found with this hold was as the father you did all of the work. You had to position by making sure there were a thousand pillows underneath the mother and surrounding the baby. The purpose of this hold or so they said was to make it possible for the mother to fall asleep and not hurt or squish the baby, I thought this was interesting. As for the cradle hold, this was where the mother pressed the baby to her breast and held it in a cradle like position, this position I found to be much easier. All I had to provide to my wife was one pillow called a nursing pillow; you can buy this at Target, Wal-Mart, or even a specialty store. But you need to make sure you buy it because it saves you a lot of time from having to rearrange pillows. In this position, the mother again can cradle and hold the child while feeding, wow are you missing being held yet? Well, don't worry, you won't after I go through a little more of this.

After learning the holds, the mother finds themselves asking questions about how comfortable nursing will be or what types of discomforts comes with nursing. All I can say is that as time goes on; your wife will start to think you were gentle with your sucking. The nurse tells the mother that after the baby latches on; it will take in a good amount of the breast and will pretty much have the nipple in the back of its throat. At this point, the baby is able to create let down for the mother and start to receive milk. Let down is where the baby has sucked for a short period of time and milk has started to flow on a more consistent basis. Yes, you are definitely at this point being let down, get use to it for about another year. As the baby starts to receive milk, the mother will produce what is needed and will provide for the child. Of course, in the first few days there is little for the baby to receive, but as time goes on, things start to happen, and now your wife looks like two gallons of milk are hanging from her chest and the enlargement of her breast start to make you think this is a good thing. Although this does not happen for a few days, the excitement of knowing this is enough for you at this point. In fact, if your wife is blessed already, you find that they can get larger and if your wife is petite and small, guys you will never want her to go back. I have heard that after child rearing that when they shrink, men have their wives go in for breast augmentations just to get them back again. I was not this type of husband, yet.

Back to our story: we sat there listening for about an hour and yes you can fill up an entire hour talking about breast feeding. As time went on, my wife learned that when she gets sore that she could use some cream made for breast feeding that will help with the soreness and if it became too bad for her to start using a breast shield. Yes, I told you it was going to get weird. A breast shield, this is like adding an extra nipple to your wife's nipple. It is a hard plastic piece that forms the nipple and has holes on the end of it for ciphering out milk. It almost looks like a plastic clear salt shaker end that came off and now is being used as protection from which your baby will suck on. It is a new innovative way of looking at your wife. After hours of finding out how hard a baby can suck and how sore your wife will be, you then ask what about pumping? Guys, all I can tell you, do not say moo or you will be hit.

Although most of you probably have never been on a dairy farm or seen a cow milked, your wife has just turned into Ms. Daisy the friendly milk supplier and she has extension upon extension on how to suck milk out of her breast. After seeing the contraption first hooked up, you find that it has two horns which are hooked to two clear tubes which then are hooked to a pump. I told my wife after seeing it for the first time that we could have made something very similar and saved some money. I mean all you really need is to have two funnels, with some refrigerator line and hook it to a vacuum cleaner. I thought about a high powered compressor then realized that this would only push the milk back into the boob and explode my wife's boobs. So I elected not to suggest that solution. But, seriously I mean we spent almost two hundred dollars on this pump and who knew how often it would get used. As you watch your wife connect it all for the first time, you think of a sci-fi movie where tubes and electrodes are all being hooked up and Frankenstein will soon be rising. It is seriously an interesting contraption to watch being used. After turning it on, you start to here the sucking noise, the nurse stated to turn it up and you start to hear swish, swish, swish going about five beats every second, again the let down phase. After a minute, my wife had successfully pumped her first tsp and she was excited. I looked at it and this is not an economic way of producing milk. Poor kid, it will definitely suffer unless something soon comes out of that thing.

After about five minutes and plenty of swishes later, my wife had gotten about an ounce. This was a huge achievement for her, and I could only sit there and wonder if more would come out. Of course, the nurse stated that this was a good amount, so we were happy. I do have to say after that first day, things start producing for us, as time went on; my wife was soon able to fill an eight ounce bottle in less than five minutes. Now we're talking, I could have run my very own dairy farm. After about a month there was plenty of milk to go around, or so you would think. All I can say is those little ones sure know how to down them some milk. After meeting with the lactation nurse, I was mostly disgusted with the whole turn of events and realized that life definitely was not going to be the same. As time went on, we continued to work with one another and realized that breast feeding was definitely the way to go. Although we had encouragement from all around and was told that it was best for the baby, we found this to be true when we priced out formula. I would rather just call it "mullah" because this is what it was a whole bunch of money and not enough to show for it. I was glad my wife was able to breast feed, but for about two months, guys I did not get a single lick or test of the new boobs. This is the other price you pay for having a wife who breast feeds. They spend all day feeding the baby and sometimes six times a day, by the time you want some you get the excuse, I am too sore or not in the mood. I even got the saying that your baby sucks on that do you really want to do like them? Let me tell you this, be careful because if given the opportunity, do not do it before feeding unless you want to know what the baby is getting and what it tastes like, let's just say it definitely is not the milk you buy at the store.

As time went on and the breast-feeding was doing better, my wife and I start talking about moving our daughter off of the boob onto a bottle. All I can say is we definitely did not think taking her off of the boob was going to be that difficult and we should have started earlier. As we went on day by day, I would start working with her in trying to get her to take a bottle. They say that the mother has a hard time giving a bottle to the baby, because the mother sends off a scent, I think it is they just want you to suffer for those nights and days while trying to take the baby off of the boob. In our case, I would try one night and get her to take a sip here and sip there even one night tried to put the bottle up to my chest and see if I could get her to take, well she did, but not the bottle. As I leaned in to give her the bottle, she went to latch on to my nipple, if it wasn't for the hair, I would have had some major issues of detachment. Lucky for me, she soon found that it was not as pleasant and left my nipples alone.

Even after another month or two, we were still unable to move her off of the boob and onto a bottle, we tried and tried, but the girl just took too much after her father and enjoyed the boob. I soon found that me offering her a bottle and providing food in other methods soon came to be insufficient and declared that I was not a boob. The only suggestion I can give someone here is to get the baby early on using a bottle so that you are not limited to just a boob. Although it is important for your wife and baby to spend time together and for the baby to breast feed or at least get the milk, it is so much more important for you to get sleep and to wean them off early on so that they do not become so attached that in ten years they are continually going after the breast. I mean this may be a good thing if it was a boy to know that he liked breast, but after a while it starts to become a little freaky of how much enjoyment they get from being latched on.

CHAPTER SEVEN

BOTTOMS UP

Finally we have gotten here, the time of truth and the time for disgust. I mean it is bad enough to have to clean yourself and keep up your own personal hygiene, but now you have to clean some alien looking being which has just been pooped out of your wife. I mean, this is the most nauseating thing I think you will ever do in your life. That is until your parents become too old and need a diaper change. Mine are not quite there in age, but in attitude they are real close. I mean just the other day, I would have sworn the same thing I got onto my one year old about, I was telling my parents to stop doing as well. Life is truly one vicious cycle, but that is totally a different story altogether.

Back to the butt cleaning: I can remember my first changing of a diaper when I was eleven years of age. I was visiting my Aunt and Uncle's house and they had three children, I would help clean up after them and help change them, it did not seem that bad, but boy was I naïve and just downright crazy at such a young age. The morning after our baby was born; I did everything I could to pass her back and forth between my wife and the nurses. At first, I had successfully completed the day of birth and did not have to change a diaper and I tell you what, the nursery at the hospital was awesome. I could call down and like room service they would take her have her changed, bathed and cleaned and did not even have to tip. I encourage all parents who are in this situation to take in the use of the nursery, because when you get home you do not have this luxury. Newborns do not eat enough to really have bad diapers and if you are breast feeding we have heard it is much better of a smell and not as bad of a diaper. Someone lied!

After getting out of the hospital, we of course were given many different types of diapers and tested each and everyone to their fullest. I am not kidding; the baby pooped so much in the first month and before you could get a new diaper on her, she was pooping again. We started off with one brand and as we were using it, we noticed that virtually every time she had a number two, she would blow out the diaper. I cleaned strollers, car seats, couches, floors, outfits, hammocks, swings, diapers, myself, and yes even the baby. No matter what we did or where we went, we always found ourselves cleaning her little bottom. If you have not put your car seat together or your stroller, wait until you have to wash or clean the cloth on it. This is such fun. They make you pull the belts out from the back unscrew 10 or 12 screws from the cloth which is where the baby sits, then you have to loosen all of the belts and slip them out of the cover and then disconnect them from the car seat, because, yes they will get this dirty also. Finally, you will then have about seven or eight pieces with about fifteen or twenty screws and then after scrubbing three times with Resolve and using everything except Clorox hopefully you finally get it out. Then if you are lucky, you wash it in the washing machine, if not you will have to wash by hand. Afterwards, you will have to wait for it to dry, put it back together and then less than two days later start the process all over again. This was our first month of diapers. Finally, after trying a few more brands and styles we were able to find the style and size which worked best for us. The diapers were still just as bad, but the squirts and leaks were not.

Although this may have been true most of the time, I can still remember that one day as my wife and I were working on making dinner and I was getting some dishes and she was at the refrigerator. She was standing there using the baby Bjorn holder, a holster that you can strap the baby to you and be able to have hands free movement. While standing there at the freezer she starts to feel this drip down her leg onto her foot. Of course preoccupied with other things, I continue to work on what I was doing, after a few seconds, I could hear my wife just shriek. At this point, my daughter had allowed herself to fill her diaper completely and because of the pressure from the Bjorn, she was compressed and it was like squeezing tooth paste out of a tube. The poop was runny and orange with a green tint and as it ran down my wife's leg, she could only stand there and continue to watch and feel as it left the diaper and landed on her. Again while I was still working on something else, I walked over to give a helping hand. In doing so, I stepped accidentally into the trail which was left behind and to my wonder it was not only on me and my wife but on most of the kitchen floor. We spent over an hour cleaning up after this episode.

As time went on, the liquidity of the poop became less and less and the solidness started to become more often. Also with a more solid bowel movement also comes with it a foul smell. We started off breast feeding and the smell was not to terribly bad at first, but as time went on it would just start creeping up on you. In fact early on and throughout our first year we found that our baby always seemed to have gas. We would give her Mylicon and gas relief drops, but boy could she fart like a sailor.

I mean there were some mornings that you would just regret even waking up. As many parents do, we sometimes allowed our child to sleep in the bed with us. As most of us guys know, our wives blame anything that sounds like a fart must have come from the father. One morning while lying in bed, I am turned over facing my wife and pretty much in the line of fire of our baby girl and as I lay there she lets a fog horn of one go. It was loud enough that I think the neighbors could hear it. As I quickly opened my eyes to the fumigation of skunk spray, I could slightly see her face and as I looked at her, she would just grin and smile as of course I always do when I let one rip. Her facial expression was just priceless, so as a father, you know then you must have done something right. Only problem is you may think that you would want her to grow out of it, but the truth is if she never did then you do not have to worry about the boy issue later in life.

Back to the smell of it all: of course, with dirty diapers there is normally a smell. The problem is I did not think it would be as hazardous as it has become. You almost wonder how in the world something that cute can cause something that smelly. I mean the first time she provided the stench; I thought that the sewer in the house had backed up. I mean it gets so bad that literally you and your wife will hide in the covers or under your shirt collars trying to avoid the smell. One day my wife and I were sitting in the living room and while watching TV, it was obvious that there had been a dead lingering smell and that she had filled her diaper. As I watched our little nine month old child move around the room, I got a strong whiff of it as she crawled by, with my wife lying down right next to me. As she passed, I lifted my collar to help block the smell, guys at this point your B.O. smells better than this. As she continued to walk around the room, I was doing everything I could to avoid changing the diaper. As I looked over at my wife, she had disappeared under her cover. As I went to pull back the cover she was pinching her nose and soon we realized something had to be done, that is before we lit a match and burned the house down. After sitting there a few more minutes debating on who would change her and who would not, we finally decided to go together and while one held the legs the other would wipe. I think that day it only took twelve wipes to thoroughly clean her little bottom, but geez it was the worst smell I think my nostrils have ever encountered. Unfortunately, this happens more and more as time goes by and even though you would like to admit that it gets easier the truth to the matter is you are just thankful you get to go to work and avoid those stinky things all day long.

Although the diapers are a terrible thing to deal with the next is the cost of these diapers. We never thought of going all natural and using cloth diapers. Although some people may decide to do this to save money more power to them! We decided to buy deposable diapers. When they are smaller they come in smaller boxes and then as they grow so does the quantity in the box until you get to fours and fives and then you kind of plateau out. Although we started off using at first only five or six diapers a day and most of them being wet only. As you transition from newborn to size ones it helps provide understanding of why they offer more diapers as your child grows, because at this point they are producing more. As you are now getting 230 diapers per box that is if you use the warehouse size, you will soon be using approximately 8 to 10 per day and out of those you will be getting at least two really bad and stinky diapers. They have gotten so bad for our family that we no longer use the diaper genie, instead we package the diaper up in a throw away bag and quickly take it outside. We used our diaper genie for the first nine months and it worked great, one of the best inventions I have ever seen. Now that the odor leaks out, it is only good for wet diapers. No more stinky for you!

Recently, we have decided to start purchasing the scoop bags for dogs because they are cheaper and although that may be inhumane, this is basically what you are doing with a child, waiting for the diaper and then scooping the poop and throwing it in the garbage. So far, we have saved approximately twenty dollars using this method and get about three times the amount of little bags. I like the ones that have the skull and cross bones on it for they truly represent what is in them. These bags come in great when you are in the car and need to throw a diaper away and enclose the stink your baby has just offered up to you. The biggest issue with doing it this way is when your wife forgets to throw away the bag after stopping at a rest area or when you come home. The next day when you get into the car, you thought something has died and are searching for a dead rodent or animal and then find the diaper in the skull and cross bones bag sitting under the car seat or possibly stuffed between the rear door and the seat. Remember it could have been worse. Not only the smell could have been there, but also without the bag, you could have had a mud pie squished between everything oozing everywhere. Now that is a sight!

As I said, as time goes by the diaper gets worse and worse, now you have diaper rash more often and have to stick your finger into your babies butt and put cream all over it. In fact, we have gotten this new butt paste called Boudreaux's Butt Paste, so now after a period of time of changing my daughter's dirty diapers I now call her Boudreaux when she needs to be changed. It is my way of getting her back for what she puts out.

Finally, the last thing you need to remember and be prepared for when it comes to bottoms up is there are foreign objects that sometimes come out of that thing you have to wipe. I mean what you thought to be green beans comes out looking like slime and what looked like mashed potatoes one day going in comes out looking like green beans. There is always a saying what goes up must come down and I say what goes in must come out. In fact, if you have a boy good luck preventing the squirting and target practice when the diaper comes off. I hear that when a boys diaper is removed he then thinks it is funny to squirt you with his little wee-wee. Well, all I can say is goggles! As for girls, they are a little slyer about it. When you feel like you are getting the hang of everything and you have been changing diapers for months and have not had a mishap that is when they get you. The other night I was changing my daughter and in the dark no less, suggestion, not a wise thing to do. As I am changing her I am wiping her butt and removing the diaper from underneath her. As I go to get another diaper, she takes it upon herself to pee all over the table. As I am putting a new diaper on her, I still do not feel the wetness and as I go to dress her for bed and lift her then everything just starts running down my arms to my chest. Yes, it had been soaked up by her outfit and when I squeezed, it was like squeezing a sponge with water in it. Of course, this is not the worst thing that can happen, but it is not enjoyable either.

Changing a baby's diaper is not a science, but it sure takes practice and what comes out looks like a fungus for which you may have seen in a science class. It is amazing how much stuff can come out a little innocent baby. After a while the word innocent will not be in your dictionary or vocabulary when describing your little one. Remind yourself that you love them and do as I did, when it smells, hand them off to the wife. Also you can invite family over often this is the only break you will get from changing these things. In fact, it is like a mini vacation. You get free room services and dry cleaning for the baby, but the sad part is the baby knows and holds out for you.

So bottoms up to you and good luck with staying clean, dry, and disinfected. You will need plenty of hand wash, sanitizer, and wipes. All of which will get you clean, but none will eliminate the smell.

CHAPTER EIGHT

THE WRAP

Now that we discussed how to change them and feed them now we are going to attempt to put them to sleep. No, I do not mean get a tranquilizer or sedative, although the thought has crossed my mind. I mean it is time to get them prepared for bed. As a newborn, we struggled with how hot and cold a baby should get while sleeping. Of course, at this early of age they are not allowed to sleep with covers or anything for which they can pull over their faces. This is important, so although you may want to smother them, please don't. Ours was born in the winter or fall season, so we decided to use the technique that the hospital taught us and that was to wrap them and swaddle them tightly. According to the nurses, this was something that could be done for quite a while because the baby felt like they were still in the womb and thoroughly enjoyed it. Of course, like normal, our baby was special, she could be wrapped but like Houdini find her way out without a problem.

We finally found this contraption that is made to look like a blanket but is sewn at the bottom to work like a cocoon. You take it and place the baby inside the bottom and with one to two folds you have the baby swaddled or wrapped. This was the best invention I have ever seen. We were able to wrap our baby and while doing so found that she somewhat enjoyed it. At first it was the only method of getting her to go to sleep. We would bathe her and cream her down, yes you will go through some cream and guys although you may have never thought that you would use cream or cream someone you will with your baby, and it is just natural. After getting her prepped we would then dress her in an outfit which would not make her too hot and wrap her. I started out wrapping her very loose thinking that it could possibly hurt her, but after about a week she was out of that and I needed to go to more drastic measures. So then I started tightening the wrap a little more. If I could get her to go to sleep before laying her down she would last like that for a few hours. As the night went on she would most definitely find her way out. So of course, I started trying different methods of wrapping her. With this said, I felt like I was back in boy scouts trying to learn how to tie knots in order for them to stay and hold. In this case no matter what I did she continued to find a way to get out of it. As time went on, we found that we struggled more and more wrapping her and as she became too big, we had to stop. This brought about a totally different problem; now that she has been wrapped for so long she had become accustomed to it. Because of this, she would not go to sleep without being wrapped. At around three months, we were still using a large blanket to wrap her up. Gradually we were able to get her out of the habit, but then she picked up new tricks to the trade. She started wanting to be rocked and held as if she was wrapped and then after that she wanted to turn on her side and lay on her back. No matter what we tried, we continued to try finding new means to getting her to go to sleep.

At this point we became desperate. We would buy soothers and mobiles and other means to help her get to sleep. There are ones that play classical music and others that play lullabies. Although these were interesting for her to look at it also stimulated her senses. Then we found night lights and tried those. We would turn them on and let her watch them, but as she did she would want to touch them and play with them so again they only prevented her from falling asleep. Then we tried her mobile, this worked for a short period of time, but as we found the time, it plays, on all of these was very short and became almost too short for it to have any effect on soothing her. After receiving three or four soothers and trying other methods of soothing, we soon tried to let her, self soothe. Yeah, whatever you read, good luck with this one. We would allow her to sit in her crib looking at the lights and hearing the music and as we watched her on her little monitor, we would watch how these things only continued to wake her. Then we tried just sitting her in her crib and letting her be in the dark, after a few minutes of screaming and three shades of red, we found that when she stopped breathing we would need to go in and calm her. I would say that we had tried everything, nothing was as effective as the original wrap and so we struggled for quite a while.

You may hear from your parents or friends how great their child is and how well they sleep, but do not believe them. I have this theory and it goes something like this. I believe that no matter what you try and no matter how good of a parent you are or what you read, it will not change the habits of your child's sleeping. I like to take what the doctor said when we first visited him, to heart. You just have a child who needs little sleep. What, I said! Of course through College and High School I needed little sleep, but now I love my sleep the more the merrier. We found that changing her schedule would help since she was a child who needed little sleep. So we started bathing her at 9:30 p.m. and soon found that by midnight she would go to sleep, yes midnight. For the first few nights this worked pretty well, of course being a sound sleeper myself, I normally did not hear her scream, so I always had to entrust my wife to give me the details of how the night went. Guys, if you are sound sleepers stay that way, if you are not; I encourage you to become one. Although this worked for a little while, we still found that she was waking every so often throughout the night. But what we did find from this was that she would sleep at least until 7 or 8 the next morning, which was nice. Of course as time passes this becomes old and you want them to start sleeping more and go to bed earlier, all I can say is day light savings time. Although it does not seem much, the change in time has become a lifesaver in our house. We have been able to move her bed time to an hour earlier and now get to bed normally by 10 or so. This has made me much happier, and it has helped me be less cranky in the morning.

So whatever you decide to do, whether it is wrap them, swaddle them, hold them, rock them, or even soothe them remember you have to find your babies special interest and work with that. If yours is like mine, food and boob are about all she cares for and sure enough with that mixture normally I can get her to bed. Although you think you may have succeeded at this, just wait until you start to wean them, then the boob is no longer an option.

CHAPTER NINE

THE IN-LAWS AND OUT-LAWS

As for most of you this is the time for truth and dare. Many of us have one or two family members for which we will encounter during our pregnancy, delivery, and have to deal with their home experiences. We each have those parents, grandparents, siblings, and other categories. In all of these categories you may have one or more who just do not know when to leave you alone, stop bothering you or simply will always get on your nerves. In my family there are none of these, we are like the Waltons, but when the lights go out, anything goes.

While in the hospital, we faced many struggles with deciding whether or not we wanted anyone in the delivery room. Each mother believed they should have the opportunity no matter whether they were in-law or biological. Let me give you some history first and then you can see where I am coming from. I met my wife when we were in College, at that time she and I were good friends and got to know each other through the Baptist Campus Ministry. While there, I really got to know her and how crazy her life was or so I thought. After a few months, we decided to start dating and behold after a few more months, felt like this was meant to be forever. At this point, I found out truly how it really was in her family and what I would have to look forward to with our life ahead. At that point, I found that her mother was a three time divorcee and her dad, or who I thought was her dad, was dating someone really seriously. As I got to know her more, I realized that something was missing. She later told me that her dad was her adoptive dad and that her biological was out of the picture. After a few months, and lots of encouraging, she decided to get to know him and for a while it was like having three dads, three moms, one step on the way, and ten new siblings. Yes, when you marry and get remarried you find that you will have biological, adoptive, and step of all sorts. Then when they all get remarried life definitely becomes confusing. After many months, we finally decided to get engaged, I asked each of her parents, this would be her mother, adoptive father, and biological father for her hand. At this time, her mother and I did not get along very well. I like to think it was because I was taking her little girl out of her life and she did not know how to handle it. The truth though is I think she just did not like me. Well, life goes on and so did ours. Although we got lots of grief from her mother, I still decided to marry her and proposed. We were to live happily ever after right?

As time has gone by, I slowly but surely started to gain the understanding of her parents, they warmed up to me, or like the saying goes keep your friends close, and keep your enemies closer. I was probably still the enemy, but at least there were no shotguns or threats made directly. Even at the wedding as her two fathers walked her down the aisle, I thought about running, but decided to go through it anyways. As years passed and we found ourselves pregnant; most would think that this would be an enjoyable experience. You start to get those same thoughts and feelings you once had when you first met. You start get these stares and looks and then the side conversations start. One grandparent does not believe that they will get enough time with the new child and the other is begging for a boy, because if it is a girl she will never see it because of course all girls go to the mother's mother. If it is a boy, the mother-in-law believes that they will not know how to relate because all she had was girls and five of them for that matter. So after Russian roulette is played with what the child's gender should be, you wonder wow that much over a 50/50 chance what happens when they do not actually get to see it every day. As time passed and we found out what the sex of the baby was going to be, we were all happy. Then the grandparents wanted to know if they will be invited to the ultrasound, although some say they don't want to be, but you know that they do. Others say they want to come, but truly you don't really want them there and the others have been forgotten and are now lost out of your life. I am telling you, I thought I had it hard until I met my wife. I only had my two parents, but adding five more became the challenge.

Again, as more time passes, you find yourself now focused on delivery and when the baby will be expected. The greatest part about having a large family is the gifts. We of course, could not have only one shower, we had to have multiple showers, one for this family and one for that and none of them could be together because of how the family was formed. So total we had about seven showers for our baby, then you add in the friends and those who love babies and want one, so they smother you until you allow them to go register you with all of the stores and visit every day to check out the size of the belly and how the nursery is coming along. Again, the showers are not that bad, that is unless you have to compare the size of your belly to that of your wife and she is nine months pregnant. This can be a little embarrassing for you at first, but then you realize that yours is a thing of pride and hard work and hers will be gone soon and you will once again be the biggest in your family. So at the showers be careful for all the games, this is just their way of suckering you into getting passionate and becoming more feminine. Guys you still need to uphold your composer and remember you are a man.

As the day approaches and you start to go to the hospital while wondering about how life will be after the baby is born. You see all of these family members and how many they are with normal everyday items, you start to think about birthdays, Christmas, Thanksgiving, and other special events and wonder how in the world are you going to juggle all of those so that you do not get scrutinized for allowing one to see the baby more than the other and so on and so forth. Then you start to think, when the baby comes out, it will be fragile, how do I prevent it from getting sick or being dropped. You may have sibling like mine and realize that it would be safer leaving the baby in the wilderness for forty days and forty nights than to let some of your siblings hold it. As you are thinking about these things, then you wonder, are you going to allow anyone in the room for the delivery. As your wife will say that is a private area and no one but the doctor will see it, this sometimes even means you guys. In our case, we enjoyed the birth of our daughter as we had discussed in earlier chapters by ourselves, we were able to allow people in afterwards, but we did get those few precious moment by ourselves before the herd was wrangled in and the room filled with utter disgust that she got to hold her first and they got a picture and we did not and so on and so forth. If you are lucky, you will live far away and you will only have to deal with people flying in or not being able to come. Do not misunderstand me, family is great to have and be around but only for a short period of time. You have to have your limits and mine is about ten minutes.

After delivery, you have all of your family member's especially immediate ones there wanting to hold the baby. The poor kid will get passed around like a hot potato for about three hours right after being born. I mean it probably thought as it came out of the womb it had it hard, well when it met this family it knew it had it harder. As the days passed less and less of the family came which kind of gave relief, but like I said you soon have to take them home. As we arrived at home, most wanted to see her arrive, so they joined at our house for the arrival and then shortly after most left. At this point, sleep is the most desired idea on your mind and no matter what people say or do, that is all you really want. So, after quickly rushing all of the family out of the door, you finally have a moment of rest. Days later you find out that this is when it starts to get tough. The phone starts to ring and because all of our family live within miles of our home, the questions of how is the baby, is she doing well, I have not seen since Monday at 3:00 and it is Monday at 6:00 now I need to know she is ok, and it all starts again the next week. Then when you visit the grandparents you start to hear "We never get to see her" and "If you want us to keep her let us know." We probably got about ten offers before we even left the hospital that they would be happy to take her home.

After a few months, we of course did not want to leave our new born child and as for being first time parents we found ourselves a little more protective. You find yourself not wanting to do the things that you once loved to do. Simply because you do not want to call one parent and ask for help when the other will certainly be jealous. As time went on, our Anniversary came and we decided to go out, of course there are rules for everything and you have to go with the person you trust the most. In this case, we decided to go with the person who we believed would listen and follow our every instruction so we went with one of my wife's sisters. I mean don't get me wrong, we know everyone loves our child from at least the family perspective, but there are just some people to whom you will feel more comfortable with leaving the child. In this case, we wanted to make sure that no one visited while we were gone and that the baby got plenty of sleep and was not fought over like a last piece of meat at the dinner table between hungry lions. Just to give you an idea of how bad it can get, let me give you a scenario which happened to us.

Our first night out away from our child was again for our anniversary. As we left the house we knew something would go wrong, but figured we would try anyways. The rules were set, no guests, just feed, and do not let anyone in the house or even answer the door. As we were leaving our house to go to the movies and after getting our tickets, we got into our movie and started watching it. After five minutes sitting there getting the first relaxation we had enjoyed in a long time, we started to hear the phone vibrate. Sure enough it was our trusty babysitter calling. Wondering what could be wrong, we answered and to our amazement, we found that yes, one of the step in-laws with one of the siblings decided to drop by. Although this would normally be ok, we had given strict rules and wanted them upheld. As a good babysitter would do, with their life threatened, they ignored the door. As the door bell continued to ring and the knocking was never ending it was certain that they would not leave. Right when I had gotten settled back into the movie, the phone vibrates again. All I can say is if you have in-laws like I do or even parents, these things are not that shocking. But give me a break. Well, I answer and sure enough those little pesky people were still outside peaking through every crevasse they could find to look through. After answering the phone, I then had to call the outsiders and give them the same lecture and rules and when it comes to family everything is personal, so good luck. As time passed, that night was easier, but it would only get worse, now I had a sibling who was mad with me and in-law who believed they did nothing wrong. So, long story short, we did not get the gift they had supposedly brought for us that night and for weeks later we did not even talk. So, depending on how your relationship is with your in-laws, one way to surely get them to leave you alone is basically to tell them where to go, if you want them in your life you must try harder to not let the little things get to you.

Like I said, although life continues and people will not understand, this is the same thing you will continue to find happens to you on a regular basis. Visiting one in-law and not the other is grounds for dismissal and possibly even loss of gifts. Inviting them all over is grounds for confusion and bickering to occur. Even simply not inviting them over or getting together with them is grounds for you to hear that you don't love us as much as you do them. No matter what you do or how often you do it there is no winning with family. You will always face those trials of not spending enough time, giving enough time or simply allowing enough time with their grandchild. There is no getting past it, it is just the way life was meant to be so deal with it or move far away.

Finally, when it comes to in-laws and out-laws, it is always wise to start early asking what people want to be called. I have found that with having so many people in our lives it will only become more difficult the longer you wait. We have a Grammie, Grandma, Papa, Granddad and soon to be many others, but I can only imagine what my child will do when she reaches the real world every person who is the age of forty or older will be a grandparent to her and those who are younger will be Aunts and Uncles. She will not know the difference and wonder if everyone in her life is truly related or what role they truly will play. I have found that even close friends sometimes wonder what they will be called. It is amazing to me that people really do worry about what their names are or how they will be addressed. I started playing with the idea of calling various people by their expressions instead of what they really wanted to be called. For my mother-in-law it would be Weizer like in *Steele Magnolias*, the movie, for she struck me as the dragon lady in the story at the end and for which the kid should be scared of. For my sister it would be hey you, and for my mother it would be Gorilla Orillia because her middle name is Orillia and she does not like it. The fun we can have with behind the scenes, decisions and calls, just wait though because I have heard what little ears hear they repeat. You may find yourself in a pot full of hot water if these names ever got out. In fact, my wife is writing this part for me for all those who are reading. This is my excuse, and I am sticking to it. In fact, I left this whole chapter to her discretion so if you are reading this and are my mother-in-law it was your daughter's idea.

CHAPTER TEN

THE MOMENT OF TRUTH

At the time of arrival you have to ask your self were you truly ready. Were you ready for the long nights and lack of sleep? Or was it only a dream? If only it was, would you wake up refreshed and relaxed when it was all said and done? The truth hits you right in the middle of the forehead as you realize nothing you are about to experience is what you could ever imagine. The joy and excitement experienced by having a new baby is one of the most enjoyable experiences I have ever been able to participate in my entire life. Although it has been a ride and adventure to this point, I know there is much to go after and accomplish, I just do not know where life will lead and what it has in store next.

The moment of truth of whether you are ready to be a father never really sinks in until the day your baby is being held in your hands. To be able to touch their head for the first time and experience the late night rocking them to sleep just becomes priceless. I realized for the first time when I truly was ready to be a father and that was the morning after our daughter was born, the shock had worn off and I was standing in the hospital room afterwards in the post partum room watching my wife sleep and my baby girl curl her fingers around my index finger. As the morning sun rose to watch her lying there realizing that this was the result of something my wife and I was able to have, it just warmed my heart and gave me unlimited joy. Of course, the day before I was wishing for her to be placed back inside my wife and looking for the receipt for a return option, but truly I knew that being a father would be an adventure all into itself.

When looking back at this past year, I realize that life has definitely given me a blessing and I owe it all to the Lord for what he has provided and we are truly blessed to have McKenzie in our life. Although there have been numerous diapers, spit ups, clothes to be washed, wipes needed, and now food to be bought, I have to truly say it has all been worth it to watch this bundle of joy grow and flourish to become a walking little tyrant that she has become today. Through the long nights of endless waking and lack of sleep to the sick days and well days, life again is just something you cannot overcome or ever compare to anything else. We have spent much time with our little girl showing and teaching her how to become the type of grownup we want her to be. We show her in how we discipline, play, hold, love, and cherish her in the time we have together. No matter what, we find ourselves constantly wanting to spend more time with her and enjoy every moment of the day with our little blessing.

Before she was born, we went with a theme idea of using Lady Bugs for her room. We found many little lady bug outfits, drapes, bedding, clocks, lamps, piggy banks, towels, hats, bathing suits, and even stuffed animals. The theme truly meets the idea of what she has brought into our life. Many people relate lady bugs to something that brings good luck. I am not into horoscopes or special meanings, but I felt this to be appropriate for this book and to give you a better understanding of how I feel about my daughter. It is said that lady bugs are also considered to be a symbol of love. It was believed that in Asian traditions, a ladybug when caught and released would faithfully fly to your true love and whisper your name in his/her ear. Upon hearing the Ladybugs message your true love would quickly without hesitation find their way back to you. The number of spots on the back of the ladybug was believed to indicate how many months would pass before this wish for love would come true.

The birth of our child has definitely brought my wife and me closer together. We have been able to fulfill our passion for loving her and our dreams and decisions of raising her together which has helped our relationship blossom into a wholesome and solid relationship. We have truly been bitten by the love bug and blessed with McKenzie in our lives. We have that connection which allows us to whisper back and forth and provide a bridge not only between us, but by being together we can build and form beautiful things. With McKenzie in our lives, we truly can see how being joined together only makes us better and how having this little bundle truly makes our lives complete.

When choosing her name, I wanted to go with something that would relate to who we wanted her to become, but to also express the thoughts and ideas of what we wanted our daughter called. When done, we came up with McKenzie Faith. The great part about this name is it provided us with both hopes about finding something that would give good strong meaning behind, but also be something we liked. The name McKenzie comes from Scottish origin, its meaning is "fair one." With this, I look at it meaning that our daughter is so beautiful and I hope that she gets her mother's looks because my wife truly is the most beautiful women I have ever seen. Also, the meaning of the name means that she is fair and just in decision making. I do hope with all my heart that when she grows to be older that she will be able to understand the difference between right and wrong and with good moral standings make the decisions for which she will have to make. Whether they are hard or easy, hopefully she will be able to make them. Finally, we gave her a middle name of Faith. My wife and I wanted our daughter to grow in the Christian value and understand what it is to be a Christian and walk in faith knowing that no matter how hard life gets that she will always have the support of her Savior, and when decided she will accept Him into her life and receive Him as the one who will provide and give her guidance when her parents are no longer capable or able. I encourage you as a father-to-be or father currently, to do likewise with your child. To look at the smallest details of your life and theirs and help guide them down the right path. Although we cannot do much for them after they leave our care and guidance, we can at least teach them to understand the values of those around them and give them the understanding that life is more than what is on this earth.

I have a lot to be thankful for. I have a wonderful wife and child. But you know it does not end there. Through this book I have shared with you my last year's journey through becoming a father and how this past year has changed my life. At the beginning we got some laughs and we realized that raising children can not only be fun, but also very rewarding. I have found that there is never a time that you should allow yourself to settle for what is easy. Instead do those things which you will be able to share with your child as they become older and provide new ways of interaction between your child and you. As a young boy, I always had this dream of changing the ways my parents raised me, I want to be that father who does things with their son and to be excited for the girl on their prom night or when they are scared provide a large area for them to crawl into and comfort them. Well for the last year, I have been doing all I can and now I encourage you to do likewise. Of course my story does not end here; I still have all of my life to work out and as long as I live to continue raising my daughter. In addition to that, something that I have been holding out for until last, I now get to try these experiences all over again. My wife decided to surprise me about two months ago that we are expecting our second child. Of course the anxiety starts all over again, but you will have a handle on it better than the first. In my case, she decided to dress my little girl up with an outfit that stated, "Big Sis." All I can say, is here we go again.

Guys hang on, although the first child came, the love life did not disappear so quickly. But protection and the pill are still recommended. I am still in shock and not certain what to do, but I do know that just like the first, I will not know all the ins and outs. No matter, what I will be able to provide love, shelter, and caring arms for my current but also my future child. Although I will struggle with not having the boob all to myself, now I have to share with two, this only means less for me, but more oh so much more to care for with the two.